The great questions of the day
will not be settled by means
of speeches and majority decisions
but by iron and blood.

Otto von Bismarck

For Max Rosett, with my unfiltered affection and respect.

Photographs © 2010: akg-Images, London: 10, 13, 25, 32, 34, 35, 42, 44, 55, 56, 58, 66, 70, 76, 81, 85, 86, 90, 93, 94 top right, 94 bottom, 95 top, 95 center, 96 top, 97 top, 97 center, 98 bottom, 98 top right, 98 top left, 99 top, 105, 108, 112, 114, 116, 118, 121; Art Resource, NY: 95 bottom (Adoc-photos), 49 (Bildarchiv Preussischer Kulturbesitz), 99 bottom (Snark); Bridgeman Art Library International Ltd., London/New York: 23 (Weltliche und Geistliche Schatzkammer, Vienna, Austria); Getty Images: 37 (Hulton Archive), 97 bottom (Richard Price), 94 top left (Time Life Pictures/Mansell); Mary Evans Picture Library: 63, 87, 96 bottom (© Illustrated London News Ltd), 21, 104; The Granger Collection, New York: 110 (ullstein bild), 82.

Illustrations by XNR Productions, Inc.: 4, 5, 8, 9
Cover art, page 8 inset by Mark Summers
Chapter art by Raphael Montoliu

Library of Congress Cataloging-in-Publication Data
Heuston, Kimberley Burton, 1960–
Otto von Bismarck : Iron Chancellor of Germany / Kimberley Heuston.
p. cm. — (A wicked history)
Includes bibliographical references and index.
ISBN-13: 978-0-531-21278-3 (lib. bdg.) 978-0-531-22824-1 (pbk.)
ISBN-10: 0-531-21278-5 (lib. bdg.) 0-531-22824-x (pbk.)
1. Bismarck, Otto, Fürst von, 1815–1898–Juvenile literature. 2. Prussia (Germany)–Politics and government–1815–1870–Juvenile literature. 3. Germany–Politics and government–1871–1888– Juvenile literature. 4. Statesmen–Germany–Biography–Juvenile literature. I. Title.
DD218.H594 2009
943.08'3092–dc22
[B]

2009009683

Tod Olson, Series Editor
Marie O'Neill, Art Director
Allicette Torres, Cover Design
SimonSays Design!, Book Design and Production

© 2010 Scholastic Inc.

1 2 3 4 5 6 7 8 9 10 R 19 18 17 16 15 14 13 12 11 10   23

A WICKED HISTORY™

Otto von Bismarck

Iron Chancellor of Germany

KIMBERLEY HEUSTON

Franklin Watts®
An Imprint of Scholastic Inc.
New York Toronto London Auckland Sydney
Mexico City New Delhi Hong Kong
Danbury, Connecticut

The World of Otto von Bismarck

During his rise to power, Bismarck defeated three powerful nations and built the powerful German Empire under the control of Prussia.

Baltic Sea

Königsberg

EAST PRUSSIA

POMERANIA

WEST PRUSSIA

E

M

P

Vistula R.

POSEN

RUSSIAN
EMPIRE

Oder R.

SILESIA

D•
ague Königgrätz

EMIA

STRIA-HUNGARY

Vienna

miles
0   100   200

0   100   200
kilometers

KEY

A Bismarck strenuously opposes the Liberal Revolution of 1848.

B In 1851, Bismarck represented Prussia at the assembly of the German Confederation.

C In 1864, two years after becoming prime minister of Prussia, Bismarck started a war with Denmark over Schleswig and Holstein.

D Prussian troops defeated Austria in the Austro-Prussian War of 1866.

E In 1871, with France about to surrender in the Franco-Prussian War, Bismarck declared the unification of German states into the German Empire.

F Bismarck died, having ruled the German Empire as chancellor for two decades.

Unification of Germany

Prussia, 1865

Added to Prussia, 1866

Added to form North German Confederation, 1867

Added to form German Empire, 1871

━━━ Boundary of German Empire, 1871

TABLE OF CONTENTS

A Wicked Web

A look at the allies and enemies of Otto von Bismarck.

Family, Friends, and Colleagues

WILHELMINA MENCKEN
his mother

FERDINAND VON BISMARCK
his father

BERNHARD AND MALVINA ("MALLE")
his brother and sister

JOHANNA
his wife

MARIE, HERBERT, AND WILHELM
his children

OTTO VON BISMARCK

HELMUTH VON MOLTKE
Prussia's chief of staff

ALBRECHT VON ROON
Prussia's minister of war

FRIEDRICH WILHELM IV
king of Prussia (1840–1861)

WILHELM I
Friedrich Wilhelm's brother;
regent of Prussia (1858–1861);
king of Prussia (1861–1888);
kaiser of Germany (1871–1888)

Rivals and Opponents

FRANZ JOSEPH
emperor of Austria (1848–1916)

NAPOLEON III
(LOUIS NAPOLEON)
emperor of France
(1852–1870)

FRIEDRICH III
son of Wilhelm I;
kaiser of Germany
(March 9–June 15, 1888)

WILHELM II
son of Friedrich III;
kaiser of Germany (1888–1918)

OTTO VON BISMARCK, 1815–1898

OTTO VON BISMARCK, THE PRIME MINISTER of Prussia, sat at dinner with his two oldest friends, looking for a way to draw France into war.

It was a good dinner. Dinners at the prime minister's house were always good. One look at how his uniform strained over his belly told the story. Bismarck loved to eat and drink. And what Bismarck wanted, he usually got.

But no one had an appetite tonight. Bismarck and his dinner guests—Chief of Staff Helmuth von Moltke and Minister of War Albrecht von Roon—were too depressed.

For years they had been trying to start a war with France. Three weeks before, it had seemed as if they had succeeded. A Prussian prince had been offered the crown of Spain. Bismarck urged the prince to accept, and when he did, the French reacted just as Bismarck had hoped. They flew into a rage. The Prussians, they claimed, were trying to surround France.

The French ambassador demanded that Prussia's king, Wilhelm I, convince the prince to reject the Spanish crown. "I owe this mess to Bismarck," King Wilhelm grumbled. Then he sent a message off to the prince, who agreed to withdraw.

The news made Bismarck and his dinner guests miserable—which may not seem like a healthy reaction to avoiding a terribly bloody war. But Bismarck had a reputation for using war to his advantage. In the past six years, he had drawn Denmark, then Austria, into battle and defeated them both. Each time, he had negotiated a peace that made the German state of Prussia bigger and stronger. If he could only draw France into war, he might unite all German-speaking people against a common enemy and draw them into a single empire that would dominate Europe.

In the middle of the somber dinner, a servant entered and handed Bismarck a telegram from King

Wilhelm. In it the king described how he had bumped into the French ambassador while on vacation. When Wilhelm had tried to say a few nice words about the end of the crisis, the Frenchman read him a list of new

BISMARCK AND HIS ASSOCIATES discuss politics. Bismarck kept both his allies and his rivals off balance, thundering about "iron and blood" at one moment and cracking jokes at the next.

demands. Stunned by the man's rudeness, the king had given the ambassador a cold goodbye and walked away.

After Bismarck read the telegram, his mood immediately brightened. He excused himself and disappeared into his study. When he returned a few minutes later, he carried the telegram in one hand and a pencil in the other. He showed Moltke and Roon the lines he had drawn through about half of the words, and read what remained. It now sounded as if King Wilhelm had insulted the French ambassador.

"If I publish this in the newspapers and send telegrams to all our embassies, Paris will hear about this by midnight . . . it will be like waving a red flag at the French bull!" Bismarck declared.

He was right. Within a few hours, headlines in Paris were screaming, "Public Insult to Our Ambassador!" With a few strokes of his pencil, Bismarck had successfully pushed France into declaring war against Prussia. Bismarck had gotten his war. And France— not Prussia—appeared to have started it.

Bismarck's bold act became the stuff of legend. All over the world, political and military leaders tried to imitate the way he coldly manipulated his friends and enemies to achieve his goals.

In the end, however, the pencil lines he drew so confidently through that telegram would prove to have more terrible consequences than anyone could have imagined.

PART 1

Forging an Iron Will

CHAPTER 1

In the Middle

Young Otto grows up caught between MOTHER AND FATHER, CITY AND COUNTRY.

OTTO VON BISMARCK WAS BORN ON A large country estate in the German state of Prussia on April Fool's Day, 1815. Prussia and dozens of other small German-speaking states lay sandwiched between three much larger countries—Russia to the east, Austria to the south, and France to the west.

As Otto grew into a sturdy red-haired little boy, he learned firsthand what it was like to be caught between rival powers.

The first great power in Otto's life was his mother, an ambitious woman named Wilhelmina Mencken. Wilhelmina had grown up at the royal court in Berlin, where she played with two little princes who would later rule Prussia. She left the city to marry Otto's father and quickly grew bored by her husband and his dull country life.

But she saw a spark in Otto. Despite the big, slow-moving body he had inherited from his father, the boy's mind was quick. Wilhelmina had high hopes for her gifted son. She pushed him mercilessly to study hard and make something of himself.

Wilhelmina's harsh manner hurt and puzzled Otto. "As a child," he later wrote, "I hated her."

The second great power in Otto's life was his father, Ferdinand von Bismarck. The Bismarcks had been noble landowners for centuries. In Prussia, such people were known as Junkers. They owned most of the land and employed poor peasants to farm it. They also staffed the powerful Prussian army.

Junker families generally sent their sons to military schools that didn't offer much academically, but did a good job turning out soldiers who knew how to follow orders.

Junkers had the reputation of being tough, unimaginative, and absolutely loyal to their king. Their tastes were simple. When they weren't away at war, they spent their time striding around their estates with hunting rifles. At night they washed down enormous meals with equally enormous quantities of beer and wine.

Otto later confessed that he was "truly fond" of his father and proud of his Junker heritage. "I am a Junker and mean to have the advantages of being one!" he declared. From the time he could walk, he spent every minute he could exploring his father's estate with two big slobbery dogs. He loved the way country people did what needed to be done without a lot of talk and worry about good manners. Most of all, he loved how well Junkers ate.

YOUNG OTTO VON BISMARCK and his friends have a snowball fight. Otto spent his early childhood years at a country estate called Kneiphof, which was in a part of Prussia called Pomerania.

Otto expected to spend his days in this agreeable way until he was 12 or 13 and old enough for military school. But his mother had no intention of allowing her son to squander his gifts. She sent him off to Berlin's best boarding school just before his seventh birthday.

Otto was miserable in Berlin. He spent time with his mother's well-connected family and played with the royal children of Prussia. But he hated everything about the school, which he said "ruined his childhood." The place was cold, and he had trouble getting out of bed in the morning. He was always hungry. The other boys, the children of more sophisticated city folk, teased him for being a Junker. The masters beat him for not doing his homework. One day he glanced out a classroom window and saw a team of oxen plowing up a field. It reminded him so much of his family's country estate that he burst into tears.

A Union of Germans

WHEN BISMARCK WAS BORN, THE AREA KNOWN today as Germany was a patchwork of 39 small and independent states, each ruled by its own prince or king. The states formed a loosely organized alliance called the German Confederation. The leaders of each state agreed to defend each other in case of war. They also agreed on common trade practices to make it easier for German merchants to do business across state lines.

Austria, with its sprawling empire, dominated the German Confederation. Prussia, thanks to its Junker soldiers, ranked second.

As Bismarck grew up, more and more people demanded that the German-speaking states become a single unified country. The problem was, what would that country look like? Would it be dominated by Austria or Prussia? Would it be ruled by a king, or by the people? It would take a man as powerful as Bismarck to provide the answers.

FRANCIS II, emperor of Austria. Like his predecessors, he dominated the smaller German states.

CHAPTER 2

Playing His Own Music

Bismarck tries to be a
"GOOD-FOR-NOTHING"
and mostly succeeds.

WHEN OTTO WAS 17, HIS MOTHER SENT
him to the University of Göttingen in the neighboring
state of Hanover. She told Otto that she expected him
to study hard and make a brilliant career for himself,
the way her father and grandfather had.

Although Otto was all for having a brilliant career,
he was not so sure about the "studying hard" part. He

was much too busy having fun to go to class. He let his red hair grow long and paraded around the city of Göttingen wearing outrageous clothes. He joined a dueling club, where members faced off with swords to prove their skill and courage. Bismarck was a fine swordsman and won almost all of his duels. He acquired a dashing scar on one cheek and was quick to explain that the opponent who'd given it to him had cheated.

He spent his evenings doing what he loved best: eating, smoking, drinking, and arguing. "No man should die before he's smoked one

AS A TEENAGER, Bismarck went to the University of Göttingen. He had a brilliant mind and was fluent in five languages. But he was more interested in partying than studying.

thousand cigars and drunk five thousand bottles of champagne," he claimed.

Bismarck tried his best to earn a reputation as a *Taugenichts*, a "good-for-nothing." But his mind was as greedy as his appetite. When he tired of parties, he would retire to his bed and secretly devour books in five languages: German, French, English, Greek, and Latin.

Only a year into his college career, Bismarck had run through so much money that his parents made him transfer to the University of Berlin, where he could save on rent by living with family. But Bismarck didn't work any harder in Berlin than he had in Göttingen—until just before it was time to take his final law exams. Then he hired a private tutor, studied around the clock for weeks, and managed to pass the exams.

It was 1836. At 21, Wilhelmina's promising son had his law degree. Now it was only a matter of finding that brilliant career.

That proved more difficult than Bismarck had hoped. He moved to the small city of Aachen to help administer territory that Prussia had recently acquired. He spent his days preparing legal documents and settling petty disputes. Before long, he'd gone nearly mad with boredom. Bismarck began to rethink his mother's plans for him. "The longest title and the most splendid decoration in Germany," he complained, "will not compensate me for the shriveled outlook which is the result of such a life."

Although his job was a disappointment, Bismarck's new home was not. Aachen was a resort town near the French and Belgian borders. Wealthy parents and grandparents vacationed there to bathe their aching joints in the hot sulfur springs. Their daughters and granddaughters came with them for the nightlife.

Fascinated by this glittering new lifestyle, Bismarck was soon up to his old tricks. He escorted beautiful young women to opera galas and champagne suppers. He ordered custom-made suits and boots—on credit. He fell in love with the daughter of an English duke and wooed her with expensive gifts—also bought on credit. Hoping to win the money he owed, he began to spend time at the gambling tables, but only lost more. The duke's daughter moved on to someone else.

Bismarck asked his parents for a loan, but they refused. His father's estates were a mess after years of mismanagement, and his mother was battling cancer. They felt it was time their son learned to stand on his own two feet.

Instead, Bismarck fell in love with another English girl. When she wanted to do some sightseeing, he got two weeks' leave from work and went along. But the time slipped by. The next thing he knew, six months had passed, and he had lost both the girl and his job. His debts, unfortunately, had not disappeared.

Even worse, like all educated Prussian men, he had to serve a year as an officer in the military. He tried to get out of it by claiming that an old dueling wound made it painful to raise his arm. The army didn't believe him. They assigned him to the garrison in Potsdam, near the king's palace. There, Bismarck spent time with the royal family, getting to know the princes, Friedrich Wilhelm and Wilhelm. Aside from that, he did as little as possible, counting the minutes until he could resign his commission.

As he explained in a letter to his family, life as a Prussian officer was like being "a member of an orchestra, but I want to play the kind of music that I like, or none at all. . . . I belong in the clean air, in the green forests, and on the good black soil."

Seventeen years after leaving the countryside of his birth, Bismarck was ready to go home.

CHAPTER 3

"God's Soldier"

Religion and marriage help Bismarck
FEEL AT HOME IN THE WORLD.

On NEW YEAR'S DAY IN 1839, OTTO'S
mother died of cancer. Otto, his brother, and his
father divided the family's estates among them. Otto
returned to an estate called Kneiphof, the site of his
happiest childhood memories. Once there, however, it
didn't take him long to realize that a lot had changed
since those carefree days.

For one thing, he now had to care for his 13-year-
old sister Malle, whom he barely knew. For another,
Kneiphof was on the verge of collapse. Everywhere

Otto looked, he saw evidence of his father's neglect. Roofs needed shingling, fields needed fertilizing, fences needed mending.

For the first time in his life, Bismarck worked hard. And before long, he actually began to enjoy it. He realized that hard labor and sweat could be as satisfying in their own way as a fragrant stew, hot fresh bread, and a stein of good beer.

Still, as the years rolled on, the attractions of country life began to dim. It was all so—predictable. Tasks he had once welcomed as challenges began to wear on him. There was money now for books and wine and trips abroad. But life seemed to have lost its flavor. Malle, whom Bismarck had grown to respect and enjoy, married and left home. Then, in 1845, his father died. A depressing "blue mist," Bismarck said, hovered between him and the rest of the world.

He tried the usual remedies. He ordered libraries of books and read them all. He left Kneiphof for his father's run-down manor at Schönhausen, which he soon had running like clockwork. He fell in and out of love. He hunted, drank, and ate. He behaved outrageously at parties, announcing his late arrival by shooting pistols into the air. Nothing helped.

Then one night he was invited to a dinner party at the home of his neighbors, the von Thaddens. The von Thaddens were members of a Lutheran sect known as the Pietists, and they took their faith very seriously. There was a long prayer before dinner and lots of conversation about the Bible during the meal.

AFTER 24 YEARS as a good-for-nothing, Bismarck seemed, for a while, to find his calling as the manager of his family's estates.

Bismarck wasn't used to all this talk about God, and he found it irritating. But there was something about the von Thaddens that intrigued him. He was particularly fond of one of the von Thadden daughters, Marie. Like Otto's sister Malle, Marie had both a gentle heart and an independent mind.

Bismarck discovered a new sense of peace at the von Thadden home. As he spent more time there, he started thinking about God and reading from the Bible every day. He also met the woman who would become his wife. Shy, dark-haired Johanna von Puttkamer was Marie's best friend. When Marie was unexpectedly stricken with typhoid fever and died a few weeks later, Otto and Johanna turned to each other for consolation. They were engaged by the spring of 1847.

Otto and Johanna made an unlikely couple. Johanna was quiet, conventional, and deeply religious. She disliked public attention as much as her husband craved it. But she would be a devoted and loyal wife who fussed over Bismarck in a way his mother never had.

JOHANNA VON PUTTKAMER and Bismarck got engaged in 1847. Johanna, Bismarck later told people, "made me what I am."

In return, his letters to her betray a tender, loving side that few people suspected he possessed. "You are my anchor on the sheltered bank of the river," he wrote. "If it should come adrift, may God have mercy on my soul."

For 32 years, Bismarck had not felt at home in the world. Now he found a new way to understand his life's purpose. "I am God's soldier, and wherever He sends me, I must go," he told his new Pietist friends. "He shapes my life as He needs it."

FARM TO FACTORY

AS BISMARCK GOT HIS PEACEFUL COUNTRY estates in order, the world around him was changing fast. New technologies had farms churning out wheat, barley, potatoes, and corn faster than ever before. All over Europe, more food was being produced with fewer farm workers.

Men and women who were no longer needed on the farm flooded into Prussia's cities. They found work at factories powered by steam engines, filled with new machines that made cloth, buttons, shoes, and other goods.

Life was different in the city. Merchants and factory workers, better educated than most country peasants, weren't tied to the Junkers' conservative ways. Many were drawn to a set of political ideas known as liberalism. They wanted democratic elections, written constitutions, and a free press—and they were willing to fight for it.

WORKERS BUILD a locomotive in a Berlin factory.

CHAPTER 4

Joining the Battle

Bismarck finds his way into politics—AND LIKES IT.

BISMARCK AND HIS FIANCÉE MAY HAVE thought they were starting a quiet life in the country together. But before their wedding date arrived, Bismarck's career as a private country landowner came to an abrupt end when he was called to duty in Berlin.

In 1847, King Friedrich Wilhelm IV, whom Bismarck had known since childhood, decided to call a diet, or temporary parliament, to discuss important issues facing Prussia. Bismarck was chosen by local Junkers to represent them at the diet.

Friedrich Wilhelm had two main goals for the diet. He wanted financial support to build a railroad so that Prussia could keep up with industrial development in neighboring countries.

He also hoped that the diet would silence the demands of liberals, which seemed to grow louder by the minute—in Prussia and all over Europe. Businessmen, workers, even liberal-leaning Junkers felt it was time for their king to start sharing power. They wanted a voice in how the country was governed. They wanted a written constitution that would limit the authority of the king. They wanted a permanent parliament whose members would be elected by the people. Friedrich Wilhelm hoped that the diet would give the liberals just enough say in the government of Prussia to make them go home satisfied and drop the most extreme of their demands.

When Bismarck arrived in Berlin in May 1847, he assumed, like the king, that the diet would be dominated by solid, conservative Junkers. He was wrong. For three days he listened in horror as delegate after delegate stood up to demand a constitution.

By the fourth day, Bismarck had had enough. He jumped to his feet to let the liberals know exactly what he thought of their demands. A colleague later remembered him as "a long, tense, slightly plump figure, with a blond beard and thin hair on top . . . spitting out his words as if in a suppressed rage." In a high, thin voice, Bismarck insisted that asking for a constitution was "an insult to Prussian honor."

The diet erupted into a storm of protest as booing delegates stomped their feet and pounded their desks in outrage. To show how little he cared about the delegates' disapproval, Bismarck turned his back on them, shook open a folded newspaper, and caught up on the day's news until things had calmed down.

To Bismarck's great satisfaction, King Friedrich Wilhelm IV sent the diet home without giving the liberals the constitution they wanted.

In July, Bismarck and Johanna went ahead with their wedding. Then the newlyweds took an extended honeymoon in Italy. Bismarck met with Friedrich Wilhelm in Venice, where the king happened to be vacationing as well. Over dinner, Friedrich Wilhelm thanked his childhood playmate for his support at the diet.

Otto and Johanna returned to their country home. But Bismarck had discovered a way out of the drudgery of country life. He couldn't wait to get back to Berlin and throw himself into politics. "I hear the trumpet," he excitedly wrote a friend. "I must join the battle. I have a natural craving for combat."

CHAPTER 5

Revolution!

BISMARCK GOES TO WAR
against the liberals.

THE KING MAY HAVE SENT THE LIBERALS packing after the diet in Berlin, but he had not defeated them. At the beginning of 1848, they rose up in force to challenge the very existence of monarchy in Europe. In the process, they gave Bismarck the "battle" he wanted.

All across Europe, liberal businessmen and aristocrats, aided by armies of hungry laborers, erupted in anger. They led a series of revolts that threatened to topple kings and queens from Rome to northern Germany.

The news began to arrive at Bismarck's estate in Schönhausen late in February. Workers had flooded the streets of Paris, forcing the French king from his throne. Three days later, an assembly in the German state of Baden demanded a bill of rights. Mass meetings and street protests spread throughout the German states. In Austria, protests forced the king to replace the conservatives in his cabinet with liberals.

In March, the revolt reached Berlin. Flying revolutionary banners of black, gold, and red, huge crowds gathered in the streets. They demanded a constitution, a parliament, freedom of the press, and a united Germany. On March 18, a crowd of demonstrators forced a tense standoff with police. Two shots rang out, and Berlin erupted into open violence. By the time the troops were called off, hundreds of protesters lay dead in the streets.

Fearing total chaos, Friedrich Wilhelm decided to make concessions. He and his ministers rode through the streets wearing the revolutionary colors. They paid

WORKERS RIOTED in Berlin's streets during the Revolution
of 1848. Bismarck offered to send peasants from his estates to help
put down the uprising. Instead, Friedrich Wilhelm decided
to negotiate with the rebels.

their respects at the cemetery where the massacred protesters lay buried. The king then promised both a constitution and a parliament full of elected representatives with whom he would share power.

In Schönhausen, Bismarck heard garbled reports from Berlin. Unwilling to believe that a mob had imposed its will on Friedrich Wilhelm, Bismarck convinced himself that the king must have been imprisoned. He raced about his estate trying to arm peasants and march them to Berlin to help put down the uprising. But when he approached the king's military leaders, they suggested Bismarck send them something they could actually use—like cabbages and potatoes.

Unable to stand by and watch the crisis unfold, Bismarck caught the next train to Berlin. On the way to the capital, he bought a new hat and shaved off his well-known red whiskers, hoping to disguise himself from the liberal mob. Bismarck dashed to the king's palace, but the guard on duty refused to admit him. Bismarck scribbled a note telling the king that he, Otto von

CROWDS FLYING revolutionary banners cheer at a parade for Friedrich Wilhelm. The king had just agreed to protesters' demands to liberalize his government.

Bismarck, had come to offer his assistance. He insisted that the guard have the note delivered immediately.

When time passed and the king did not appear, Bismarck had to retreat. He hung around Berlin for a while with other conservatives, trying to convince the king to take back his promises to the liberals. Friedrich Wilhelm refused.

By the summer of 1848, liberals seemed to have won the day all across Europe. In capitals from Paris to

Rome, Vienna, Prague, and Berlin, monarchs reluctantly agreed to share their power with elected parliaments. For the first time, ordinary people would have a say in the laws they had to obey and the taxes they had to pay.

Bismarck was beside himself with frustration. As he looked back over the last few months, it seemed he had been humiliated at every turn. Johanna, who was expecting their first child, urged him to give up his political career and return to Schönhausen.

But Bismarck had no intention of quitting politics. The conservatives desperately needed someone to speak for them, and he was convinced he was the man for the job. Before the summer was out, Bismarck had organized Prussia's first conservative political clubs and its first conservative newspaper. He wrote articles and gave speeches that were so shockingly rude that they became the talk of Berlin. By the time his baby girl was cutting her first teeth, her daddy had become, in his own words, the "best-hated man in Prussia."

PART 2

Blood and Iron

CHAPTER 6

Hating Austria

Bismarck joins the diplomatic game AND MAKES A POWERFUL ENEMY.

IN 1849, BISMARCK HAD HIS BUSIEST YEAR yet. He got himself elected to the new Prussian parliament, or *Landtag*, which was more conservative than the liberals had hoped. He contributed anonymous articles to the newspaper he had founded. And although he found public speaking "a torment," it didn't stop him from publicly attacking the liberal cause whenever he got the chance.

THE "BEST-HATED MAN IN PRUSSIA," as Bismarck described himself, spoke urgently and tirelessly against liberal reforms.

If Bismarck learned a lesson from Friedrich Wilhelm IV's response to the uprisings of 1848, it was that most people are too weak and ineffective to be trusted with real power. He was convinced that Prussia needed strong leaders like himself, and he tried his best to convince the king to give him an important political post.

It was going to take a lot of convincing. Friedrich Wilhelm was an upright, mild-tempered man who despised Bismarck's aggressive ways. Bismarck's tactics, the king said, "smelled of blood."

In 1851, however, Bismarck's persistence paid off. The king needed an ambassador for the *Bundesversammlung* (Federal Council), a kind of super-parliament for the alliance of states known as the German Confederation. Bismarck was overjoyed to be named to what he described as "our most important diplomatic post"— especially since he had no diplomatic experience at all.

The Bismarcks packed up their family and moved to Frankfurt, the independent city-state where the Federal Council met. As part of his new job, Bismarck had to entertain frequently. One guest remembered his home as "one of those houses where everyone does what one likes. . . . Here there are young and old, grandparents and children and dogs all at once; eating, drinking, smoking, piano-playing, and pistol-firing (in the garden), all going on at the same time. It is one of those establishments where every earthly thing that can be eaten or drunk is offered you."

Bismarck devoted as much energy to his day job as he did to his dinner parties. His main task at the

Federal Council was to grapple with the Austrians for power within the Confederation. Austria was by far the largest and most powerful of the German-speaking states. The Austrians held the presidency of the Federal Council and were able to control many of its decisions. But Bismarck felt that Prussia's strength and proud military tradition should earn it at least an equal say in German affairs.

Bismarck quickly grew to resent the arrogance of his Austrian counterparts and did everything he could to stand up to them. When their ambassador took off his coat to work in his shirtsleeves, so did Bismarck. When the Austrian took out a cigar, so did Bismarck— before demanding a light from his rival. When the Austrians kept the Prussian delegation waiting, Bismarck simply left.

At one point, some of Bismarck's colleagues tried to push Prussia into an alliance with Austria against neighboring France. Bismarck growled at them: "The Austrians invariably cheat at cards and always will. I do not see how we can expect ever to make an honest alliance with them." Bismarck seemed to want a showdown with the great Austrian Empire.

Around this time, another idea began to appeal to him. Unlike many Germans, Bismarck had never wanted the German states unified into a single nation. Most of the support for unification came from the liberals, the only group Bismarck seemed to hate as much as the Austrians. "We are Prussians and want to remain Prussian," he had thundered in Prussia's parliament.

Now he began to rethink his position. Perhaps he had been thinking too small. What if the German states *did* unite into a single nation, one that excluded—and was able to dominate—the Austrians?

Bismarck's rivalry with the Austrians had driven him to an ominous conclusion. "Germany is too small for both of us," he wrote.

C H A P T E R   7

"In Cold Storage"

Bismarck becomes an ambassador—
and is sent FAR, FAR AWAY.

As HIS YEARS IN FRANKFURT WORE ON,
Bismarck's restlessness returned. It maddened him
to be serving under men whom he considered less
competent than himself. Prussia needed a strong,
decisive leader to claim its rightful place in Europe,
he believed. Whenever he got the chance, he pestered
Friedrich Wilhelm IV to name him foreign minister
so he could orchestrate Prussia's rise to power over its
neighbors. The king refused, arguing that Bismarck
was too aggressive to be effective. To get Bismarck

53

off his back, the king offered him a lesser job, which Bismarck turned down.

In 1857, Friedrich Wilhelm suffered a stroke. The next year, his brother Wilhelm was named regent and given control of the kingdom. Kindly Wilhelm was 60 years old and had never expected to rule Prussia. He found Bismarck's relentless arguments unsettling, but his advisers told him that Bismarck was too valuable to dismiss. So Wilhelm did the next best thing—he made Bismarck ambassador to Russia.

Bismarck was bitterly disappointed. He wrote a friend that the regent was "putting me in cold storage." It didn't help that Wilhelm had given important promotions to two of Bismarck's closest friends. Helmuth von Moltke was named chief of staff for the Prussian army, while Albrecht von Roon became the Prussian minister of war. Bismarck set off for Russia sure that his career was over.

Bismarck arrived in the Russian capital of St. Petersburg in the spring of 1859. He took an immediate dislike to the cold, rainy climate. He also hated his job, which required very little of him and paid even less. At least one colleague claimed that Bismarck made no attempt to hide his sour attitude. "My new chief is a man with no consideration for others," the colleague grumbled. "He makes his own policy . . . he does not entertain here, complains it is too expensive, does not get up till eleven or half-past in the morning, spends the day in his green dressing gown, takes no exercise, drinks a lot, and curses Austria."

Bismarck gradually grew to like St. Petersburg. But in 1862, he heard a rumor that Wilhelm,

WILHELM TOOK CHARGE of Prussia after Frederick Wilhelm suffered a stroke. Both men were calm and cautious, and both distrusted Bismarck.

who had become king after his brother's death, was about to name Bismarck foreign minister. Bismarck raced back to Prussia without pausing to pack, dismiss his servants, or even collect his family. He skidded into the palace at Berlin only to discover that Wilhelm was nearly as indecisive as his brother. Bismarck tried to wait patiently, but it wasn't in his nature. At last he

BISMARCK'S CARRIAGE struggles through the snow outside St. Petersburg. At first, Bismarck was miserable in Russia. He hated the food and was bored by his job.

gave the king an ultimatum—appoint him to a new job within 48 hours, or he was going home to his country estates. The strategy backfired. The king gave Bismarck a post—but it was ambassador to France.

France! Bismarck was furious. Next to liberals, Austrians, and Russian food, there was nothing he hated more than the French. "France is a nation of zeros, a herd; they have money and elegance, but no individuals," he fumed. Nevertheless, he stomped off to Paris.

He arrived in the early summer of 1862, just as most government officials were leaving the hot, smelly city for vacations in the country. Bored and restless, Bismarck decided to play tourist. He set off for London, where he was invited to a dinner with Benjamin Disraeli, an important politician who would eventually become Britain's prime minister. When a guest asked Bismarck for his opinion on German unification, he entertained himself by telling the absolute truth, confident that everyone would assume he was joking.

AS AMBASSADOR TO FRANCE, Bismarck was restless. He was eager to return to Prussia and continue his quest for power.

"You ask what I think of German unity? When I take charge of Prussian foreign affairs, I shall declare war on Austria, dissolve the German Confederation, conquer the middle and smaller states, and give Germany unity under the control of Prussia," he said.

Most people at the table broke into laughter.

His host, however, was not laughing. What Bismarck had described sounded more like an empire than a peaceful union of friendly states. Disraeli muttered to a companion, "Watch that man. He means every word he says."

CHAPTER 8

The Only Man for the Job

Bismarck becomes prime minister and explains why his opinion matters MORE THAN THE LAW.

BISMARCK WAS IN NO HURRY TO RETURN to work. He spent a relaxing summer touring the French countryside and flirting with the young wife of a friend.

The news from Berlin must have contributed to Bismarck's good mood. A crisis was developing that could force the king to call on Bismarck for help—and give him the position of power he had been craving for so long.

King Wilhelm's primary military advisers, Moltke and Roon, had long been telling him that the Prussian army needed attention. It had too few soldiers, they insisted, and its weapons were outdated.

Wilhelm, who had been a soldier all his life, went to the *Landtag* and asked its delegates to approve increased spending on the army. In 1862, however, most of the delegates were liberal businessmen and professors. They hated war, distrusted the Junkers who controlled the military, and relished the chance to challenge the king's power. To Wilhelm's astonishment, they refused his request.

Wilhelm dissolved the parliament and called for new elections. But voters chose representatives who were even more liberal than before. The king and his parliament were at a standoff. It was a true test of the arrangement that had been worked out after the unrest in 1848. According to the new constitution, the parliament had the right to approve government spending. But did they really have the power to control the future of the Prussian army?

Moltke and Roon told Wilhelm that there was only one man tough enough to break the deadlock: Otto von Bismarck. The king resisted the suggestion for as long as he could. Bismarck "would turn everything upside down," he worried. But the king also did not want to give in to the *Landtag*.

On September 16, 1862, Wilhelm decided he had no choice. He asked Roon to send for Bismarck, who rushed eagerly to Berlin. Within a week, the king had named Bismarck prime minister of Prussia with responsibility for foreign affairs.

Two weeks later, Bismarck waited to make his first speech to the *Landtag* as their new prime minister. He was excited and proud, but unexpectedly nervous. Nevertheless, he had a job to do. When his turn came, he surged to his feet, a tall and commanding presence. He gave a speech that would be remembered long after the sound of his high, thin voice had faded. "It is not to Prussia's liberalism that Germany looks, but to its power," he proclaimed. "The great issues of the day will be decided not by means of speeches and majority

AS PRIME MINISTER, Bismarck immediately made it clear that he'd do whatever it took to have his way—even if that meant breaking the law.

resolutions—that was the mistake of 1848—but by iron and blood!"

But the delegates, most of whom believed firmly in speeches and majority rule, still refused to support the military improvements.

King Wilhelm cringed when he read Bismarck's words in the newspaper. It was just the kind of angry confrontation he had feared. But in the end, Bismarck managed to get what the king had wanted. Bismarck went right ahead and collected taxes. Then he spent the money on the military without approval from the *Landtag*. Still in its infancy, the *Landtag* did not have the power to stop him.

Bismarck knew perfectly well that what he had done was illegal. But he didn't care. He practiced what he called *Realpolitik*—the politics of realism, in which what *works* matters more than what is *right*. Breaking the law and disturbing the peace, he said, "are matters of perfect indifference to me. All I care for is the well-being of my king and country."

CHAPTER 9

Man with a Plan

BISMARCK SETTLES IN AS PRIME
MINISTER and ponders how to
make Prussia a powerhouse.

Now THAT HE WAS PRIME MINISTER, Bismarck's life fell into a pleasant routine. He moved his family into the prime minister's official residence in Berlin. He typically slept late and then went straight to his office without getting dressed. His day started with the morning papers, which he read on the couch in his office.

When he finished reading, he would summon one

BISMARCK WAS OBSESSED with finding a way to protect
Prussia from Austria, France, and the other great powers of Europe.
He often wrestled with this problem long into the night.

of his aides and dictate reports and letters, pacing the
room with his hands thrust into the pockets of his silk
dressing gown. Although he was impatient with his
employees, he could also be very funny. He often made
his secretaries laugh so hard they would have to put
down their pens so they didn't splatter ink all over the
documents.

Politicians like Bismarck got a lot of their work done at social occasions. But Johanna disliked going out, and Bismarck always worried that the food and wine his hosts offered would be inferior to his own. They eventually solved the problem by doing all their socializing at home. After supper, the women would withdraw, and Bismarck would send for wine, light up a big Havana cigar, and settle in for a long discussion with his associates. He often worked more in his study after they went home.

But no matter how late he went to bed, Bismarck found it hard to sleep. He was constantly worried about the fate of his country.

So far, the powerful Prussian army had defended its borders effectively. But that was no guarantee for the future. France, Russia, and the sprawling Austrian Empire could call on huge populations to fill their armies. Tiny Prussia drafted a high percentage of its young men into the military—and it still could not field as many soldiers as its neighbors.

What would happen if those neighbors were to join forces and invade? All of Prussia could be crossed by rail in a matter of hours.

If Prussia was to have a secure existence, it had to get bigger—a lot bigger. And the best way to do that, Bismarck reasoned, was to unify the German states into a single strong nation under Prussia's leadership.

But how could he convince the other German states to trade their independence for Prussian rule? And how could he force Prussia's powerful neighbors to permit this major shift in power?

Bismarck wrestled with the problem for some time. He thought about it during the early morning hours when he could not sleep. He thought about it as he wandered up and down the green avenues of his walled garden, walking stick in hand. He thought about it as he inspected his estates at Kneiphof and Schönhausen, his dogs panting happily at his heels.

Eventually, a plan began to form in his mind.

CHAPTER 10

A Convenient War

Bismarck picks a fight with Denmark—AND STARTS A WAR.

A YEAR AFTER HE BECAME PRIME MINISTER, Bismarck took his first step toward asserting Prussian power in Europe. In 1863, the Danish king, Christian IX, announced that he wanted two mostly German-speaking states to become part of Denmark. Schleswig and Holstein lay on his southern border. Danish kings had long had a claim on the two states, but they were not officially part of Denmark.

PRUSSIAN TROOPS storm the Danish fortress at Als. The war was a triumph for the Prussians, and it exhausted their Austrian allies.

Bismarck, of course, opposed the idea, as did most other German leaders. He immediately set out to persuade the Austrians to join Prussia in declaring war on Denmark. Publicly, he said he wanted to punish Denmark for its insult to the German states. Privately, he hoped the war would weaken the Austrian army.

The Austrians fell into the trap. In February 1864, a combined Austro-Prussian force of 56,000 soldiers stormed into Schleswig.

Thanks to Bismarck's efforts to modernize the army, the Prussians fought with brand-new breech-loading rifles. They could fire five rounds in the time it took the Austrians and the Danes to fire and reload once.

Still, superior weapons did not seem to help the Prussians during the first weeks of the war. Their commanding officer, an elderly Junker named Wrangel, allowed the Danes to retreat behind a line of heavy fortifications. For two months the war bogged down into a stalemate.

Bismarck sent urgent messages to his king, begging him to replace the doddering Wrangel with Moltke. Wilhelm agreed, and shortly after Moltke's arrival, Prussian and Austrian troops smashed through the Danish defenses. The Danes withdrew to the island of Als, outside of German territory. Diplomats met to begin negotiating a peace, and the war seemed to be over.

General Moltke was not finished, however. While the negotiators talked, word came of an astonishing Prussian victory. Moltke had secretly loaded his troops onto hundreds of flat-bottomed boats and stormed Danish positions on Als. The Danes, caught unaware, lost ten times the number of men as the Prussians. The peace was renegotiated in Prussia's favor.

By the terms of the treaty, Prussia and Austria each took responsibility for one of the states they had conquered. Bismarck quietly arranged for the Austrians to take Holstein, while the Prussians took Schleswig. Since Holstein lay between Prussia and Schleswig, Austria had to allow Prussian soldiers and officials to pass through Holstein on their way to Schleswig.

In the celebrations that followed, few people considered the difficulties this arrangement might cause. And virtually no one guessed that the difficulties were part of Bismarck's plan.

CHAPTER 11

The Seven Weeks War

Bismarck takes on Austria—and
THE BODIES STACK UP.

THE DANISH WAR HAD GIVEN BISMARCK exactly what he wanted. Acquiring Schleswig and its seaports had made Prussia larger and stronger than ever. The success was all the sweeter because it had cost his Austrian allies more than they could afford. Although the Austrian emperor, Franz Joseph I, ruled a vast portion of Europe, his people were poor and his army was worn out.

With the first part of Bismarck's plan accomplished, he moved on to the second phase. It was time to expose Austria as a danger to the other German states and offer Prussian leadership as protection.

The key, once again, lay in Schleswig and Holstein. In order to get to their new posts in Holstein, Austrian officials had to pass through Prussia. Bismarck instructed his men to make life as miserable, inconvenient, and humiliating as possible for their Austrian guests.

When the Austrians began to behave the same way toward Prussian travelers, Bismarck pretended to be outraged. He claimed that he had to have a way to get his troops safely to Schleswig. Then he sent Prussian soldiers to occupy Holstein.

Furious, Austrian Emperor Franz Joseph asked the other German states to help him force Prussia out of Holstein. Bismarck loudly objected. He warned the other states in the German Confederation that Austria would come after them next, and urged them to join forces with Prussia. Many of the German states agreed.

In June 1866, three Prussian armies advanced southward into Austria. In a surprise move, divisions from a fourth army invaded three of the German states that backed Austria—and defeated them. Within the first week of the war, Austria lost more than 27,000 men and most of its allies. But Emperor Franz Joseph refused to surrender.

On July 2, two Prussian armies totaling about 124,000 men confronted the main Austrian army near Königgrätz, in the Austrian state of Bohemia. The Austrians, 205,000 strong, had taken up a defensive position on a hill surrounded by open ground.

Bismarck, King Wilhelm I, and General Moltke rose before dawn and made their way through pouring rain to a hill overlooking the battlefield.

The Prussians attacked at first light and were easily driven back. A Prussian officer remembered the sight of Bismarck during the battle. "Mounted on a huge chestnut horse, wearing a great cloak, his great eyes gleaming, he reminded me of tales I had been told in childhood about giants of the frozen north," the soldier said.

But Bismarck was not as brave as he looked. As he watched the Austrians mow down wave after wave of Prussian infantry, Bismarck felt a familiar queasiness in his sensitive stomach. If Prussia were to lose, he knew his career was as dead as the white-faced soldiers lying on the battlefield before him.

KING WILHELM I AND BISMARCK observe the
Battle of Königgrätz. The Austrians began the day with about twice
as many soldiers as the Prussians. But the Prussians were better
armed and organized, and they routed the Austrians.

Bismarck had no gun. He decided that if the Prussians lost, he would ride into the fray and get himself killed. Better death than defeat.

King Wilhelm was also uneasy. "Moltke! Moltke! We are going to lose the battle!" he fretted.

Moltke, calm as always, answered that the Prussians would win not only the battle, but the entire war. A few hours later, he was proved right. Wilhelm's son, Crown Prince Friedrich, arrived just in time with an army of reinforcements. With fresh troops in the field, the Prussians surrounded the Austrians and forced their commander to surrender.

Bismarck's triumph seemed to be complete. But as he rode out onto the battlefield among the broken bodies of his soldiers, he could think only of his own son. "It makes me sick when I reflect that Herbert may be lying like that some day," he said. "It was a sight to freeze the blood in the veins—horrible, bloody, never to be forgotten."

CHAPTER 12

About Face

While building a new confederation, Bismarck BEFRIENDS SOME OLD ENEMIES.

BISMARCK RETURNED TO BERLIN AND surveyed the results of his victory. Austria had agreed to give up all influence in northern Germany. The German states north of the Main River would form a new North German Confederation largely under Prussian control. For now, the southern states remained independent. But if Bismarck had his way, they too would one day join, forming a single Prussian-led German nation that would rival any empire in Europe.

Bismarck was a hero in Prussia. His former liberal enemies had been won over by his triumph at Königgrätz. The *Landtag* voted to give him a magnificent new estate as a token of their gratitude. He would never need to worry about money again.

Satisfied but exhausted, Bismarck limped home to Johanna in September 1866. The experience at Königgrätz had touched a soft spot in the hardened politician's heart. "Anyone who has ever looked into the glazed eyes of a soldier dying on the battlefield," he wrote, "will think hard before starting a war." Bismarck spent three months tramping through the countryside he loved before he could get on with his public life.

Near the end of 1866, Bismarck returned to Berlin and attacked the work at hand: building the North German Confederation. He sat down and studied the Constitution of the United States. Then he hammered out his own for the confederation. A North German parliament, with elected representatives, met to approve it.

Like the *Landtag*, this new parliament was

dominated by liberals—businessmen, professors, and landowners who wanted democratic reforms. In the past, Bismarck had been the sworn enemy of the liberals. Now things had changed. He desperately wanted the new confederation to work, and he needed the liberals to make it happen.

Bismarck, the crotchety old Junker, began to act like a liberal. He worked with the North German parliament to adopt the secret ballot, which would allow peasants to vote without their landlords watching over their shoulders. He passed criminal laws that would apply equally to everyone in the confederation, rich or poor. He also approved a common currency, common weights and measures, and other common trade practices to help merchants do business throughout the German states.

Bismarck's old conservative friends didn't know what to think. The man they had always counted on to put the liberals in their place seemed to have become a liberal himself. "This leaves us in a daze," said one of Bismarck's former allies.

Bismarck's efforts to strengthen the new German confederation also alienated another powerful leader. Napoleon III, emperor of France, was furious to find a new alliance gaining strength right on his eastern border. For centuries, France's great wealth had allowed it to dominate Western Europe. What right did an obscure little country like Prussia have to upset Europe's balance of power? Something had to be done to set things right.

By 1870, it looked as though that something would be war. And that was just fine with Bismarck. The independent German states to the south lay directly between France and the North German Confederation. If France attacked Prussia and

EMPEROR NAPOLEON III
of France was threatened by the
increasing power of Prussia.

IN THIS GERMAN editorial cartoon from 1867, Bismarck (right)
is depicted as a shepherd protecting his flock of German lambs
from the lion, Napoleon III of France.

its allies, these southern Germans would have to
decide which side to support—the North German
Confederation, or the invading French.

Bismarck knew quite well which side they
would choose.

C H A P T E R   1 3

The Franco-Prussian War

ANOTHER BLOODY CONFLICT
knits the German states together at last.

IN JULY 1870, BISMARCK MANAGED TO bring France and Germany to the brink of war. At a dinner in Berlin with his Chief of Staff Helmuth von Moltke and Minister of War Albrecht von Roon, Bismarck carefully reworded a telegram from King Wilhelm. Bismarck made it seem as though Wilhelm had insulted the French ambassador. After dinner,

Moltke made a bold prediction about the coming war. Prussia, he said, would win as easily as it had won the so-called Seven Weeks War with Austria.

The war officially began on July 19, when Napoleon III declared war on Prussia. During the first few days of the conflict, the disorganized French army seemed determined to prove Moltke right. French officers were sent one place while their men went somewhere else. The ammunition they needed traveled to a third location. Once they got everything to the right places, the generals couldn't agree on a strategy. They kept their armies waiting at the German border for four days while they argued over their next move.

The confusion in the French army gave Moltke plenty of time to mobilize his well-drilled troops. The Germans sent 380,000 men marching into France before the 230,000-man French army could invade the German states.

The fighting began on August 6. The first few battles were inconclusive, although the French

HELMUTH VON MOLTKE, an experienced general, led the Prussians and their German allies in the war against France.

lost more soldiers than the Germans. A few weeks into the war, however, someone in the French War Office made a huge mistake. French newspapers somehow discovered the French battle plan, and printed it!

Bismarck could barely control his delight. Knowing what the French had planned, Moltke quickly rearranged his battle formations. At the Battle of Sedan on September 1, the German army surrounded and captured almost half the French army, including Emperor Napoleon III himself. The French defeat was so complete that tender-hearted King Wilhelm was overwhelmed by the news. "Ah, the brave people," he said sadly, over and over again.

The war seemed to have ended, just as Moltke had

AFTER LOSING battle after battle, Napoleon III and his army were surrounded by the Prussians near the French town of Sedan. On September 2, 1870, the emperor surrendered, along with 100,000 of his troops.

predicted, in less than seven weeks. But the French people weren't ready to give in. Liberals in Paris, furious at Napoleon's mishandling of the war, ousted their emperor. They formed a new government and refused to make peace with the Prussians.

When Bismarck heard that the French would not accept defeat, his good sense deserted him. He tried to convince Moltke to bomb Paris into rubble. Moltke pointed out that the world would probably not approve if they slaughtered thousands of civilians and destroyed one of Europe's greatest cities.

Bismarck calmed down and settled for a siege. German troops surrounded Paris and blocked all

STARVING FRENCH TROOPS devour one of their horses. During the siege of Paris, the Prussians prevented food from going into the capital.

supplies from entering the city. There would be more fighting in the north of France. But with Paris encircled and slowly starving to death, it was only a matter of time before the French gave in.

Now that victory seemed to be near, Bismarck attended to the task that would soon become the crowning achievement of his life: the unification of Germany. He and King Wilhelm moved into the famed palace at Versailles, just outside of Paris. From there, Bismarck oversaw negotiations to bring the three main states in southern Germany—Württemberg, Baden, and Bavaria—into a united Germany. He promised them some concessions. Bavaria would control its railways and its army during peacetime. Bismarck also bribed Bavaria's King Ludwig with enough money to build an absurdly expensive castle.

By November, all the details were in place. Otto von Bismarck stood on the verge of creating a nation.

CHAPTER 14

A United Germany

Germany is born in the midst of
BICKERING AND WAR.

ON JANUARY 18, 1871, KING WILHELM I,
Bismarck, and officials from many of the German
states gathered at the glittering Hall of Mirrors in
Versailles. There, they proclaimed the creation of a
new force in Europe: the German Empire.

The new nation offered something to everyone
within its borders. The liberals had their parliament,
or *Reichstag*, with its members elected by popular vote
and granted the authority to approve or reject new
laws. Wilhelm was given the title of *kaiser*, or emperor,

GERMAN TROOPS MARCH into Paris. In the background is the
Arc de Triomphe, a monument to French military power.

though his power was mostly symbolic. Real power
rested in the hands of a single official—the chancellor
of Germany. The chancellor was responsible for all
state business. He had the power to declare war, devise
a budget, and propose new laws. The chancellor was
the true ruler of Germany, and there was only one man
powerful enough for the job: Otto von Bismarck.

The ceremony at Versailles should have been a moment of great triumph for Bismarck. But it was not a festive occasion. Wilhelm was convinced that "kaiser," or emperor, was a watered-down title that conveyed less power than "king of Prussia." At the very least, he insisted, his title ought to be changed from "German Kaiser" to "Kaiser of Germany." Bismarck nearly burst with frustration. The states had already signed off on "German Kaiser," and he refused to budge. By the time the king gave in, Wilhelm and Bismarck were not on speaking terms.

"The imperial birth was difficult," Bismarck wrote to Johanna. "As midwife I frequently felt the urge to become a bomb and explode so that the whole edifice would sink into ruins."

A few days after the tense ceremony, news came that Paris had surrendered at last. The peace settlement, however, was deeply disappointing to Bismarck, who felt the conditions were dangerously harsh. Moltke and the other generals insisted on seizing two French provinces, Alsace and Lorraine, to protect the security of the German border. They also wanted a huge fine imposed on France to pay for German war expenses. Kaiser Wilhelm supported the generals, and Bismarck reluctantly gave in to their demands. The French were forced to sign the Treaty of Frankfurt, and Bismarck went home to brood. With a treaty like that, he feared, the French were sure to seek revenge sooner or later.

By the summer of 1872, Bismarck had become one of the most powerful men in Europe. The new German Empire rewarded him with generous gifts. Wilhelm made him a prince. Bismarck and his family moved out of the cramped prime minister's residence in Berlin and into a true palace. They were given yet another large country estate—30,000 wooded acres near Hamburg. Bismarck could now count himself as one of the wealthiest landowners in the country.

Despite the fame and fortune, Bismarck claimed to be weary of public life. "There is no remedy against the approach of old age," he complained. "I am tired,

IN 1871, BISMARCK was made a prince and given the vast estate of Friedrichsruh. As chancellor, he was the most powerful man in Germany, and perhaps the most feared man in Europe.

and while I am still bound to the life of this world, I am starting to sense the appeal of contemplation and rest. What I would prefer is to leave the stage for a spectator's box."

Like it or not, however, there was more drama to come—and Bismarck was destined to play a leading role.

Otto von Bismarck in Pictures

YOUNG JUNKER

Otto von Bismarck was born into a family of Junkers—landowning nobles with a long military tradition.

OTTO MARRIES

Bismarck married Johanna von Puttkamer in 1847. Their marriage lasted until her death, more than 45 years later.

COUNTRY BOY

After his father's death, Bismarck, who had been a failure up to that point, worked hard to manage his family's estates.

REVOLUTION

The Revolution of 1848 shocked Bismarck. It forced Prussia's king to allow a constitution and an elected parliament.

OUT IN THE COLD

In 1858, Bismarck was named ambassador to Russia. Wilhelm, the new regent of Prussia, wanted him out of the way.

ODD COUPLE

Bismarck (left) thought King Wilhelm I (right) was too soft to be an effective ruler. Wilhelm thought Bismarck was dangerously reckless.

OTTO CRACKS THE WHIP

When Bismarck became prime minister, he announced that Prussia would rule by "iron and blood." He quickly gained a reputation as a fierce bully.

DRESSED FOR SUCCESS

Bismarck served only one year in the military—and hated it—but he understood that Prussia's strength was its army. He usually dressed in a general's uniform when he appeared in public.

EMPEROR OF FRANCE

In 1870, Napoleon III made the mistake of personally leading the French armies into battle against Prussia, even though he was a military amateur.

TRIUMPH AT SEDAN

During the Franco-Prussian War, Napoleon III was captured along with 100,000 of his troops in September 1870.

A REAL FAIRY TALE

Bismarck was willing to make deals with the southern German states to get them to join his confederation. To King Ludwig of Bavaria, he gave the funds to build Neuschwanstein (left)— which became one of the models for Disney's Sleeping Beauty Castle.

PAPER EMPEROR

Wilhelm is crowned German Emperor at the Hall of Mirrors in Versailles. The title of emperor was largely ceremonial—real power would be held by Bismarck.

THE ENEMIES WITHIN

No sooner had Bismarck built an empire than he started to identify enemies within it. He targeted Catholics first, then socialists.

BLOOD, IRON, AND ... COMPROMISE?

In the last two decades of his career, Bismarck set out to establish himself as an "honest broker" who worked to keep the peace in Europe.

BEST-HATED MAN IN EUROPE

As this cartoon from a French newspaper shows, Germany under Bismarck was viewed as a super-power with an unlimited appetite for gobbling up other regions—maybe even the moon.

SACKED!

In 1890, the new emperor, Wilhelm II, announced that he intended to run the empire himself—and fired Bismarck.

PART 3

Ruling an Empire

CHAPTER 15

Enemies of the Reich

Bismarck argues with the Catholic Church—AND LOSES.

In THE SUMMER OF 1871, BISMARCK gathered his strength and threw himself into the task of governing the new German nation. He had brought more than two dozen states and 40 million people together. Now he had to keep it all from falling apart.

His first big problem came from the Catholic Church. When the southern German states joined the empire, they brought a huge population of German

Catholics with them. Many of these Catholics had opposed unification with the largely Protestant northern states. They owed their loyalty first to the pope—then to the German chancellor. Their representatives in the *Reichstag* stood ready to oppose Bismarck's attempts to take power away from the states and centralize it in the new German government.

Bismarck set out to make sure the Catholics understood that the German state always came first. His fight with the Catholics became known as the *Kulturkampf*, or culture struggle. It started in 1871, when Bismarck made it illegal for priests to discuss politics from their pulpits. The following year, he banned religious teachers from public schools and sent government inspectors into religious schools. In 1873, he pushed the so-called May Laws through the *Reichstag*. These new laws gave the government control over the training and licensing of priests.

Catholics all across Germany were furious. In the elections of 1874, the Catholic Center party doubled its

BISMARCK IS SHOWN as a bullfighter wrestling with Pope Pius IX, head of the Catholic Church. Bismarck argued that Germans' first loyalty should be to the government, not to their religion.

strength in the *Reichstag*. Bismarck was booed when he made an appearance there. In July, he was visiting the town of Bad Kissingen when a young Catholic shot at him with a pistol. The bullet merely grazed Bismarck's hand, but the would-be assassin had made his point.

Still, Bismarck plowed ahead. In 1876, he introduced a law banning criticism of "the family, property, universal military service, or other foundations of public order, in such manner as to undermine morality, respect for the law, or love of the fatherland." He also closed dozens of Catholic monasteries, convents, and schools.

It soon became clear that the *Kulturkampf* was a big mistake. Forced to choose between loyalty to their church and loyalty to the state, most German Catholics chose the church. Every time Bismarck passed a law

BISMARCK SURVIVES an assassination attempt. The shooter had been enraged by Bismarck's anti-Catholic laws.

meant to weaken the Catholic Church, the Catholic Center party won more votes.

In 1877, Bismarck told Johanna that he was "weary of life." The late nights, the huge meals, the endless drinking and smoking and worry had taken their toll. Bismarck was only 62, but he looked much older. He was overweight and his teeth were rotting, although he refused to see a dentist. He had constant pain in his stomach and bowels.

In April, Bismarck told the kaiser that he needed a break and left Berlin for his estates. He spent nearly a year taking long, thoughtful walks through the countryside, his dogs at his side. He had tried to bully the Catholic opposition, and he had failed. For the first time, it occurred to him that force didn't always work.

CHAPTER 16

Threat from the Left

Bismarck finds A NEW
ENEMY—the socialists.

Otto von bismarck had never
liked change.

Unfortunately for him, Germany was changing faster
than ever. By 1878, huge factories were sprouting up
along the Rhine River, each one staffed by thousands of
workers. Thanks to a public education system that was
open to all, most workers learned to read and write. They

were free with their opinions, unlike the eager-to-please peasants Bismarck knew from his estates. Even sleepy Berlin was changing as railway lines, electric lights, and tall buildings elbowed their way into the city center.

Bismarck, now 63 and in increasingly poor health, tried his best to ignore it all. He refused to tour the vast new factories. He would no longer travel at all except between his estates and Berlin. When

FACTORIES BEGAN to dominate the landscape of Berlin. The Industrial Revolution—and the socialist movements that emerged during this era—disturbed Bismarck.

people sent him books explaining the new world the Industrial Revolution had created, he piled them in his cellar, unread.

But there was one aspect of the new industrial world that Bismarck couldn't ignore—socialism. Factory workers wanted better working conditions and higher pay, and Germany's Social Democratic Party promised to fulfill their demands. Socialist power in the *Reichstag* was growing, much to Bismarck's dismay.

In the spring of 1878, two acts of violence convinced Bismarck that the socialists posed a serious danger to Germany. On May 11, Kaiser Wilhelm was enjoying a carriage ride through Berlin with his daughter. Neither one paid much attention to the shabbily dressed man who approached their open carriage. Then they heard a loud noise—and another—and a third. By the time Wilhelm and his daughter realized that they were being shot at, the attack was over. Their guards had wrestled the gunman—an unemployed plumber—to the ground and the danger had passed.

Three weeks later, Wilhelm was driving near the same place when shots rang out from an open window. This time they found their mark. The kaiser was so badly injured that it was feared he might die.

Bismarck blamed both incidents on the socialists. In typical fashion, he rammed a law through the *Reichstag* that closed socialist newspapers and banned socialist meetings. But, as with the *Kulturkampf*, the harsh

KAISER WILHELM IS ATTACKED by a former socialist. Wilhelm was unharmed, but a second assailant badly wounded him just a month later.

laws only won sympathy for Bismarck's opponents. At the next election, the socialists won more seats in the *Reichstag* than ever.

Then Bismarck had a brilliant idea. "Give the workingman the right to work as long as he is healthy, assure him of care when he is sick and maintenance when he is old," he urged the *Reichstag*. "If the workers have no more reason to complain, socialism will wither away."

Over the next decade, Bismarck, the wealthy conservative, enacted some of the world's first laws that provided government benefits to working people. He forced employers to help fund health insurance for employees and provide support for anyone who got hurt on the job. He also launched a national pension plan for retired workers, funded by the government, employers, and employees.

Bismarck's clever strategies preserved the new German Empire, but cost him dearly. Nearing the end of his career, he grew isolated and suspicious, convinced that he was the only one who understood what needed

AFTER SO MANY years in power, Bismarck had made countless enemies. He had also begun to take his allies for granted and increasingly treated them with disrespect.

to be done. As the years wore on, everyone from the kaiser to Bismarck's few remaining friends grew weary of the tantrums, ultimatums, and smashed crockery that were Bismarck's response to not getting his way. As his old friend Roon wrote sadly to his nephew, "The more we are sincerely attached to him, the more deeply and painfully do we feel the ethical failings in his mighty character."

CHAPTER 17

Deserted

After ruling the Germans for three decades, BISMARCK IS FINALLY FORCED ASIDE.

BY 1883, BISMARCK'S HEALTH WAS SO BAD that Johanna decided that something must be done. She summoned Dr. Schweninger, the man who had saved the kaiser after he had been shot.

Bismarck did not want some old fool telling him what to do. When the doctor began to ask him about his symptoms, he snapped, "I don't like being asked questions."

BISMARCK RELAXES at a country estate with his wife, some friends, and Dr. Schweninger (standing, third from left). Under the doctor's care, Bismarck said he felt better than he had in 20 years.

"Then get a vet," Schweninger snapped back. "He doesn't question his patients."

Schweninger was the first and last person who Bismarck ever allowed to bully him. The doctor oversaw his meals, exercise, and even his bedtime. The results were startling. Bismarck lost 50 pounds and most of the aches and pains that had begun to take over his life. He even went to the dentist.

In 1888, Bismarck's old ally Wilhelm I died. The German throne passed to his son, Friedrich III. When Friedrich died just three months later, his son Wilhelm became Kaiser Wilhelm II.

Bismarck had known the new kaiser since childhood. In many ways, he still thought of Wilhelm as a baby and treated him that way. The old chancellor continued to make all state decisions on his own, without consulting or informing Wilhelm. That was not a wise decision.

Kaiser Wilhelm II had little use for his grandfather's bossy old chancellor. He told a friend he intended to "let the old man snuffle on for six months, and then I'll rule by myself."

One February morning in 1890, the young kaiser visited the Bismarck home. The elderly chancellor, caught unaware, received his emperor in his pajamas. Wilhelm's message was as unwelcome as his early arrival: He wanted Bismarck to resign, effective immediately. When the kaiser announced his chancellor's resignation two days later, he added, "I am

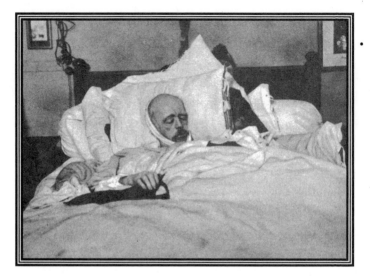
BISMARCK BREATHED his last on July 30, 1898. This
photo was taken the following day.

now the officer on watch. The course remains the same.
Full speed ahead!"

Bismarck was beside himself with fury at being
"cast . . . off like a servant." He retired to his estates
and dictated self-serving memoirs. "He will not admit
to having been involved in anything that failed, and he
will not allow that anyone other than himself made a
contribution," his secretary complained.

In the end, Bismarck's attempt to rewrite the past could not save him from an unhappy end. His faithful Johanna died in 1894 at the age of 70. He wrote his sister a few weeks later that, "What was left to me was Johanna, spending time with her, the daily question of her contentment, the sense of thankfulness with which I look back over 48 years. And today everything is bare and empty."

Otto von Bismarck died four years later, on July 30, 1898, full of bluster to his last breath. Just before he lost consciousness, a caretaker tried to spoon some liquid from a glass into his mouth. Pushing the spoon aside, Bismarck cried "Forward!" Then he grabbed the glass and drank its contents down.

A RETIRED BISMARCK poses with his loyal dogs. After his beloved wife died in 1894, Bismarck spent his last years vainly waiting to be restored to power.

꿍꿍꿍꿍꿍꿍꿍꿍꿍꿍꿍

Wicked?

꿍꿍꿍꿍꿍꿍꿍꿍꿍꿍꿍

Although Bismarck wouldn't have been surprised to be called "wicked" by his enemies, he surely would have disagreed. As far as he was concerned, he was the best thing that ever happened to Germany. Without him, in fact, there would be no Germany.

As a politician and a statesman, Bismarck acted according to a philosophy that became known as *Realpolitik*. He believed that politicians and governments pursued their own interests rather than lofty ideals. And that was just fine with him. The end, he believed, justifies the means. As he said in a speech to the *Reichstag* in 1881, "My aim from the first moment of my public activity has been the creation and consolidation of Germany, and if you can show a single moment when I deviated from that magnetic needle, you may perhaps prove that I went wrong, but never that I lost sight of the national aim for a moment."

Creating and sustaining Germany gave shape and purpose to Bismarck's life. But the cost was high. Near the end of his life, Bismarck admitted, "Had it not been for me there would not have been three great wars; 80,000 men would not have perished; and parents, brothers, sisters would not be in mourning. But that is something I have to settle with God."

The cost was higher than the lives lost on the battlefield. It was higher than the constant personal and political betrayals Bismarck made in order to accomplish his goal. In the short run, he taught his people that one way of solving Germany's problems was to go to war. When the socialists began to assert themselves during Wilhelm II's reign, some historians say the kaiser manufactured a war against Germany's enemies, just as Bismarck had done so many times. The war was World War I, which killed more than two million Germans and ended in disaster for Germany.

World War I, awful as it was, was not Bismarck's only legacy. By his actions he taught his countrymen

THIS 1915 FRENCH CARTOON, which shows a statue of Bismarck surrounded by corpses, places some of the blame for World War I on Bismarck's shoulders.

the most inhumane of all philosophies: that the road to human greatness required an entire nation to sacrifice its own perceptions, insights, and judgment to the power of one man. In the words of one historian, "Bismarck makes Germany great, but the Germans small."

Forty-three years after Bismarck and Johanna moved out of the Chancellery in Berlin, another chancellor moved in: Adolf Hitler. Like Bismarck, Hitler didn't trust the inefficiency of democracy. And like Bismarck, Hitler promised the Germans that he would do their thinking for them. The result was the atrocity that was World War II.

Timeline of Terror

1815

1815: Otto Edward Leopold von Bismarck is born on a Prussian estate.

1847: Bismarck marries Johanna von Puttkamer and is elected to the Prussian legislature.

1848: Bismarck defends the king's authority when revolutions break out across Europe.

1851: Bismarck becomes a delegate to the German Confederation's parliament in Frankfurt.

1858: Bismarck is named ambassador to Russia.

1862: Bismarck is named ambassador to France. Six months later, he becomes prime minister.

1864: Prussia and Austria go to war against Denmark over the provinces of Schleswig and Holstein.

1866: Prussia defeats Austria in the Seven Weeks War, and the North German Confederation is created.

1870: Bismarck provokes the Franco-Prussian War.

1871: Germany is unified into an empire led by Wilhelm I, with Bismarck as chancellor.

1871–78: During the *Kulturkampf*, Bismarck campaigns against Catholics.

1878–90: Bismarck's anti-socialist laws outlaw most socialist meetings and newspapers.

1883: Bismarck passes a health insurance law for workers. It's followed by an accident insurance law in 1884 and an old age pension in 1889.

1888: Kaiser Wilhelm II succeeds to the throne upon the death of his father, Friedrich III.

1890: Bismarck is dismissed by Kaiser Wilhelm II.

1898: Otto von Bismarck dies at the age of 83.

1898

GLOSSARY

aristocrat (uh-RISS-tuh-krat) *noun* a member of the highest social rank in a society

assassin (uh-SASS-in) *noun* a person who murders a well-known or important person

chancellor (CHAN-suh-lur) *noun* the name for the head of Germany's government from 1871 to 1945

chaos (KAY-oss) *noun* total confusion

city-state (SIT-ee STATE) *noun* a city that with its surrounding territory forms an independent state

confederation (kuhn-fed-er-AY-shun) *noun* a union of states, provinces, or people

conservative (kuhn-SUR-vuh-tiv) *noun* in politics, a person who stresses the benefits of tradition

constitution (kon-stuh-TOO-shuhn) *noun* the system of laws in a country that state the rights of the people and the powers of the government

cynic (SIH-nik) *noun* someone who believes that people are motivated only by self-interest

delegate (DEL-uh-guht) *noun* someone who represents other people at a meeting

democratic (dem-uh-KRAT-ik) *adjective* describing a political system in which the people choose their leaders in free elections

diet (DYE-uht) *noun* an assembly of delegates who meet to discuss political issues

diplomat (DIP-luh-mat) *noun* a person who represents his or her country's government in a foreign country

embassy (EM-buh-see) *noun* the official place in a foreign country where an ambassador lives and works empire (EM-pire) *noun* a group of regions that have the same ruler

ethical (ETH-ih-kuhl) *adjective* morally correct

Junker (YOON-ker) *noun* a member of the privileged, militaristic, landowning class in Prussia

liberal (LIB-ur-uhl) *noun* in politics, a person who favors change and reform

negotiate (ni-GOH-shee-ate) *verb* to work toward an agreement through discussion

parliament (PAR-luh-muhnt) *noun* the group of people who have been elected to make the laws in some countries

pension plan (PEN-shuhn plan) *noun* a plan make money payments to someone who has retired from work

prime minister (PRIME MIN-ih-ster) *noun* the head of government in a country with a parliamentary system; most countries with prime ministers have both a head of government (the prime minister) and a head of state (such as a king)

Realpolitik (ray-AHL-pohl-uh-TEEK) *noun* a German term for a system of politics based on practical rather than ethical considerations

revolution (rev-uh-LOO-shuhn) *noun* an uprising by the people of a country that changes the country's system of government

socialist (SOH-shuhl-ist) *noun* a person who favors an economic system in which the production of goods by factories, businesses, and farms is controlled to a high degree by a government

typhoid fever (TYE-foid FEE-vur) *noun* a serious infectious disease, caused by germs in food or water, characterized by high fever and diarrhea

ultimatum (uhl-tuh-MAY-tuhm) *noun* a final offer or demand that threatens punishment if rejected

unification (yoo-nuh-fih-KAY-shun) *noun* the process of being united or made into a whole

FIND OUT MORE

Here are some books and websites with more information about Otto von Bismarck and his times.

BOOKS

Blashfield, Jean F. **Germany (Enchantment of the World, Second Series)**. New York: Children's Press, 2003. (144 pages) *Information about the history, people, and geography of Germany.*

Farmer, Alan and Andrina Stiles. **The Unification of Germany 1815–1919 (Access to History)**. London: Hodder & Stoughton, 2001. (234 pages) *Examines the developments that led toward Geman unity, Bismarck's rise and fall, and the policies and changes within Germany up to the formation of the Weimar Republic in 1919.*

McGowen, Tom. **Frederick the Great, Bismarck, and the Building of the German Empire in World History**. Berkeley Heights, NJ: Enslow Publishers, 2002. (128 pages) *Tells the story of two powerful Prussian leaders and their contributions to the rise of the German Empire.*

Smith, Bonnie G. **Imperialism: A History in Documents (Pages from History)**. New York: Oxford University Press, 2000. (175 pages) *Analyzes politics in Europe, including the German Empire, from 1850 to 1945.*

Ullrich, Volker. **Bismarck: The Iron Chancellor**. London: Haus Publishing, 2008. (158 pages) *A short but well-written biography that includes a helpful timeline.*

WEBSITES

http://encarta.msn.com/encyclopedia_761571668/Otto_von_Bismarck.html
MSN Encarta's online encyclopedia article on Otto von Bismarck.

http://news.bbc.co.uk/2/hi/europe/142376.stm
A BBC news article about how today's Germans feel about Otto von Bismarck.

http://www.bbc.co.uk/history/historic_figures/bismarck_otto_von.shtml
The BBC's online profile of Otto von Bismarck.

For Grolier subscribers:

http://go.grolier.com/ searches: Bismarck, Otto von; Prussia; William I; Schleswig-Holstein; William II; Franco-Prussian War; Junkers; Germany, history of

INDEX

AUTHOR'S NOTE AND BIBLIOGRAPHY

The first time I can remember hearing about Bismarck was in a wonderful course I took in high school from Mrs. Pat Swinney-Kaufman called From Bismarck to Hitler. Finally, someone who got things done! And he had a long and happy marriage besides! And he wasn't Hitler! What wasn't to love?

My AP European History students seem to agree. They find Bismarck's willingness to choose a course and then never vary from it an attractive quality that seems both forthright and effective. But the experience of writing this book helped me see the laziness and pride underneath his quick, bold intelligence. What's sad but true is that by refusing to hold himself to the same high standard that he required of those around him, he damaged the well-being not only of himself and those he loved, but of untold millions in Prussia and beyond. It's a shattering legacy.

The following sources have been most useful in telling Bismarck's story.

Apsler, Alfred. **Iron Chancellor: Otto von Bismarck**. New York: Messner, 1968.

Beran, Michael Knox. **Forge of Empires 1861–1871: Three Revolutionary Statesmen and the World They Made**. New York: Free Press, 2007.

Feuchtwanger, Edgar. **Bismarck**. New York: Routledge, 2002.

Gooch, G. P. "Bismarck's Legacy." **Foreign Affairs**. July 30, 1952.

Hamerow, Theodore S. **Otto von Bismarck: A Historical Assessment**, 2nd ed. Lexington, MA: D. C. Heath, 1972.

Lermann, Katherine Anne. **Bismarck. Profiles in Power**. New York: Pearson Longman, 2004.

Lowe, Charles. **Bismarck's Table Talk**. London: Grevel, 1895.

Schurz, Carl. **Reminiscences of Carl Schurz, vol 3**. New York: McClure, 1908.

Sempell, Charlotte. **Otto von Bismarck**. New York: Twayne, 1972.

Williamson, D. G. **Bismarck and Germany 1862–1990**, 2nd ed. New York: Longman, 1998.

—Kimberley Heuston